Lynn Huggins-Cooper

Contents

CW00515967

Introduction

Key Stage 1 National Tests

Children between the ages of 5 and 7 (Years 1 and 2) study Key Stage 1 of the National Curriculum. Between January and June of their final year in Key Stage 1, (Year 2) all children take written National Tests (commonly known as SATs) in English and Mathematics. They also take part in tasks which are assessed as part of their classroom work. The tests and tasks are administered and marked by teachers in school. The test papers are also externally moderated to make sure that they are assessed consistently.

The tests and tasks help to show what your child has learned during Key Stage 1. This will help you and your child's teacher to find out whether your child is reaching national standards set out by the National Curriculum.

Understanding your child's level of achievement

The National Curriculum divides standards of performance in each subject into a number of levels, from 1 to 8. On average, children are expected to advance one level for every two years they are at school. By the end of Key Stage 1 (Year 2), your child should be at Level 2.

If your child is working at Level 1, there will be some areas of English that they need help with. If your child is working at Level 3, they are doing very well, and are exceeding the targets for their age group. The table shows how your child should progress through the levels at ages 7, 11 and 14 (the end of Key Stages 1, 2 and 3).

	7 years	11 years	14 years
level 8+			☐
level 8			■
level 7			■
level 6		☐	☐
level 5		■	☐
level 4	☐	☐	■
level 3	■	■	■
level 2	☐	■	■
level 1	■	■	■

☐ Exceptional performance

■ Exceeded targets for age group

☐ Achieved targets for age group

■ Working towards targets for age group

The Tests in English

The National Curriculum divides English into three areas or Attainment Targets. These are 'Speaking and Listening', which is assessed through classroom work, and 'Writing' and 'Reading' for which there are written tests.

The Writing Test
Your child will be required to carry out a piece of independent writing. This may take a variety of forms, including a story, a piece of 'information' writing such as a report, a set of instructions, a book review or a letter.

Spelling
This will be assessed through your child's independent writing and by a spelling test.

Handwriting
Your child's handwriting will be assessed from independent writing or by copying out several sentences of original written work.

The assessments of these areas of your child's work will be put together to give an overall Writing level. A separate level for Spelling will also be reported to parents.

This book covers the areas of writing that will be tested during your child's Key Stage 1 SATs. The topics and activities are appropriate for children working at Levels 1–3. Most children will achieve Level 2. The book has been designed for you and your child to work through together, so that you can assist and support your child at every stage. The *Test Yourself* pages give you and your child a chance to assess progress and to address any areas that need development. The activity pages may be returned to again and again to practise and consolidate skills.

Extension to Level 3

A child who achieves Level 3 will have written in a well organised manner. The work will show imagination and clarity of expression. The writing will be correctly sequenced chronologically and the sentences will normally be grammatically correct. Spelling of common words, including those with more than one syllable, will generally be correct. Punctuation will be accurately used, including capital letters, full stops and question marks. The handwriting of a child working at Level 3 is joined and the letters are well formed.

How will this book help

- This book provides the essential knowledge needed by your child to tackle the Writing tasks and tests with confidence.
- This book revises work your child should be doing in class. It does not attempt to teach new material from scratch.
- The *Parent pages* and *Notes to parents,* featured on the children's pages, offer advice to enable you to work with your child, helping to improve understanding.
- The book is designed to help your child prepare for the tasks and tests. It includes activities to help with vocabulary development, sequencing, writing in different styles, spelling, punctuation and handwriting.
- The tests (*Test Yourself* pages) allow your child informal practice for the kinds of tasks and tests included in the National Tests.
- Answers are provided on page 32 to enable your child to learn from mistakes.

When helping your child, remember the 'little and often' rule! Children working in Key Stage 1 are still quite young and may be tired after a demanding day at school. Make sure that the atmosphere is relaxed when you carry out the activities, and be ready to stop when you feel your child is becoming tired or frustrated. Above all, the activities in this book have been designed to provide a fun way of learning the skills and knowledge necessary for your child to produce the best possible work in the National Tests.

1 Word pictures

Do you like drawing? Did you know that you can 'draw a picture' with words?

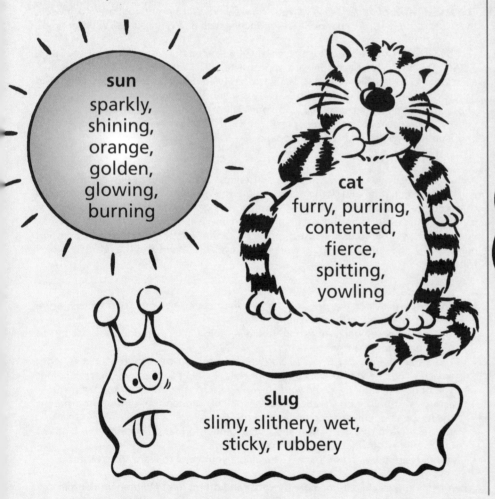

sun
sparkly,
shining,
orange,
golden,
glowing,
burning

cat
furry, purring,
contented,
fierce,
spitting,
yowling

slug
slimy, slithery, wet,
sticky, rubbery

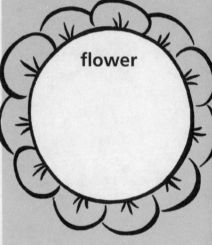
---

2 Word collectors

Sometimes when you are reading, you find words that you like the sound of, and would like to remember. Read the words Sunita has stuck on her bag:

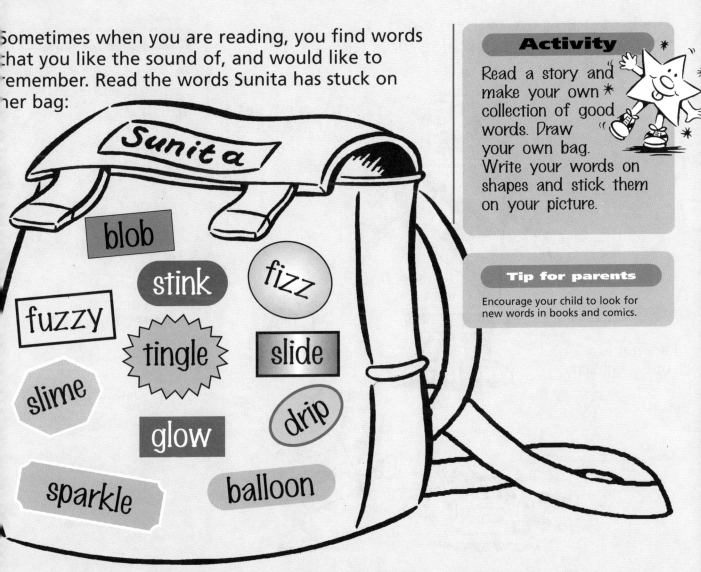

Activity

Read a story and make your own collection of good words. Draw your own bag. Write your words on shapes and stick them on your picture.

Tip for parents

Encourage your child to look for new words in books and comics.

Notes to parents

To help your child develop a varied vocabulary, encourage the collection of unusual and interesting words or phrases from the books you read together. You could use a notebook with pages labelled alphabetically.

Encourage your child to write the word or phrase on the correct page. This will also help with spelling.

3 Make your stories more exciting

The best stories use exciting words. Can you help the robots to think of exciting ways to describe themselves?

I am not just BIG but ... huge,

I am not just LITTLE but ... tiny,

I am not just SAD but ... unhappy,

I am not just HAPPY but ... jolly,

Question

What other words can you think of for **horrible**?

4 Make your own comic strip!

Do you read comics? They tell stories with pictures. These pictures tell the story of *Goldilocks and the Three Bears*. Number them in the right order, then use them to help you write the story.

Activity

Choose another story you know well. Draw boxes and draw pictures inside them. Use the pictures to write the story.

Much too small! Oops!

I'm tired

Mmm! Lovely

I wonder who lives here?

Look! Who's this?

Oh!

What a mess!

Tip for parents

You can further practise sequencing skills by writing out a simple chronological story in sentences on a piece of paper. Cut the paper into strips and let your child can arrange them in order.

Notes to parents

Your child's ability to sequence events chronologically in written work will be part of the SATs assessment. This 'comic strip' activity will help to develop this ability.

When your child has thought of another well-known story to re-tell in comic strip form, give some help with picking out the most important events to include in the strip. This could have more or less than six boxes.

5 Brainstorming

When writers are planning a new book, they often collect all their ideas together. You can do it too, before you write a story.

Here are some ideas for a story about a cat:

chases birds
miaows and yowls
naughty, steals food
fuzzy face
sleeps all day

Here are some ideas for a story about going to the fair:

lights in the dark field
getting lost
bumper car ride
ghost train ride
candy floss sticking to my face
coconut, winning one

Activity

Now write your own Brainstorm Bubble. What will your story be about?

Tip for parents

Remind your child that, for brainstorms, sentences are not necessary. Words and ideas are enough!

Notes to parents

For the SATs writing task, your child will be expected to plan before beginning to write. This brainstorming activity will help your child to 'gather thoughts together', collect words and phrases to use in the story and rough out the main events. A 'Brainstorm Bubble' is for random jottings as ideas occur to your child, before attempting the plan on page 9.

6 Story plan

Look at the story plan Dominic has filled in:

Get your story started!

Where does it happen?
On a rocky beach. Lots of things left by the sea like seaweed and shells.

Who is in the story?
A boy and his sister. Pirates. A talking fish in a bottle.

What is the exciting beginning?
Dominic kicked the seaweed. He could smell rotten old fish. Suddenly he kicked a sparkling blue bottle and heard a clink! Then he heard a voice.

What happens next?
A talking fish says he will grant Dominic three wishes if he will set him free.

A good ending
The pirates were chased away by a huge purple sea serpent.

Activity

Now ask for some paper and write a plan for your own story.

Tip for parents

Remind your child to use lots of good describing words. Suggest looking back at pages 4, 5 and 6 for ideas and at the word notebook, if your child has started to keep one.

Notes to parents

Look at favourite story books together and identify the different elements of the story. Who is it about? Where does it take place? What happens in it? This will help your child to develop the ability to plan stories. Try to help your child to write an exciting beginning that will engage the reader, and a strong ending, better than '... and then we went to bed/had our tea/all lived happily ever after.'

7 Story starters

Charlotte has used these story starters to begin her own stories.

• The spider spun madly in the corner of a dark, damp cellar. Spinderella had decided to spin the most beautiful web that had ever been seen. It was shiny and silky. Now she wanted to decorate it. She set off to look for something beautiful to put on it.

• The teddy had been forgotten. He lay behind the boxes, covered in cobwebs. The children in the house were too old to play with teddies any more. Teddy decided to find a new family. He started to climb up the dusty cellar stairs. He wondered what he would find when he got to the top and opened the creaking door.

Activity

Now it's your turn. Use one of these ideas to start a story. Don't forget to use the story plan on page 9.

* Bethany heard a strange, scrabbling noise coming from the hedge. It might just be Grendal, her cat, hunting in the grass ... or it might be something else. Bethany peered nervously into the hedge.

* Mark walked along the road to school. He had walked this way many times before, but this morning, instead of cars, there were shiny silver spaceships. Instead the people he saw every morning, there were lots of odd creatures walking and slithering along the pavement!

Tip for parents

Remind your child to use the story plan before beginning to write the whole piece.

Notes to parents

Read the story starters through with your child: they contain interesting language to motivate your child to finish the story. It is important that your child is able to plan a story before writing, ensuring that ideas are in a logical sequence, and that a variety of interesting vocabulary is used.

What did you think?

Mia has written on this caterpillar about a book she has read. Use the other spaces to write about your own books.

Title: My Hen is Dancing
Author: Karen Wallace
Best part of story:
When the hen lays big brown eggs.
Favourite character:
The cockerel because he is noisy.

Title:

Author:

Best part of story:

Favourite character:

Title:

Author:

Best part of story:

Favourite character:

Title:

Author:

Best part of story:

Favourite character:

9 Be an expert!

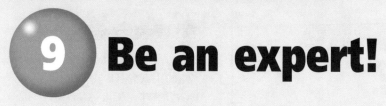

You can write your own non-fiction book. This means a book with information in it. Hassan has chosen to write about frogs. Look at the plan he has filled in.

Book Plan Subject: Frogs

Some questions about my topic that I would like to answer:
What do frogs look like?
What do baby frogs look like?
What do frogs eat?
Where do frogs live?

What sort of illustrations will I have?
pencil drawings, pictures cut from my old wildlife magazines, wax crayon picture

Ideas for my cover:
collage of a pond made with scraps —
I will use bubble wrap to make frogspawn

Title: All about frogs
Author: Me!

10 Make a snake puppet

Writing instructions

Have you ever made a puppet from an old sock?
Here are the instructions for making a snake puppet.

You will need:
an old sock
sticky paper shapes
coloured wool
glue
felt pen

1. Put the sock on your arm and mark the places for the eyes with the felt pen.

2. Tuck the sock in between your fingers and thumb. This will be the snake's mouth. Make a mark with the felt pen to show where to stick the tongue.

3. Take the sock off your arm and glue round paper shapes onto the 'eye' marks.

4. Glue a pointed shape into the snake's mouth.

5. Glue wool in patterns on the snake's back.

6. Leave your snake to dry! When she is ready, you can put on a show for your friends.

Activity

Have you ever made a mask from a paper plate? Which of these things would you use?

glue, scissors, paper, wool, fabric, pencils, coloured crayons.

Make your mask, then write the instructions telling someone else how to do it.

Start like this:

How to make a mask from a paper plate

You will need:

Tip for parents

Let your child look at simple recipes then try making the food, following each step.

Notes to parents

Help your child to practise instructional writing by going over the instructions orally. See if your child can organise ideas into logical steps.

If your child finds this difficult, repeat the activity again and ask your child to write the correct instruction for each stage while making the mask.

11 Write a letter to a friend

We write letters every day. Sometimes we write to our friends. Read the letter David has written to his friend Raj.

Activity

Practise writing your address.

15 Copper Lane
Wealden
Sussex
BN12 8AW
3rd June

Dear Raj,

Lots has been happening here! Yesterday, the baby rabbits all escaped from their hutch. When I opened the door to the shed, they were bouncing around like rubber balls! It took me a long time to catch them all! Last week we went to Waterworld and I had a go on the biggest slide. I was a bit scared, but it was fun! When you visit us, Mum says we can go again. Write soon.

Love,
David.

Tip for parents

Remind your child that letters to friends and family can include stories about what has happened. Exclamation marks can be used to show when something funny or surprising happened. The correct way to end is 'love' or 'from' or 'love from'.

Notes to parents

Letter writing is difficult for children in Key Stage 1. Look at books with letters as part of the story, such as The Jolly Postman books by Allen and Janet Ahlberg. When your child is writing a letter, try to emphasise the layout, where to put the address, where to put 'Dear ...', etc., and don't worry too much about the length of the letter to start with.

12 Write a letter of enquiry

You have seen David's letter to his friend Raj on page 14. This letter is different. David is writing a letter to someone he does not know.

15 Copper Lane
Wealdon
Sussex
BN12 8AW

5th June

Dear Madam,

My Mum and I saw a poster about birthday parties at Waterworld when we came for a swim last week. I am seven next month and I want to find out how to have a party at Waterworld. Mum says I should ask for a booking form. Could you send me one?

Thank you.

Yours faithfully,
David Byrne.

Activity

Where would you like to hold your birthday party? On a piece of paper, write a letter to the place you have chosen. Ask for information about holding parties there.

Tip for parents

Extend the activity on this page by writing a reply to your child's letter asking for information. Encourage your child to write back to make a booking.

Notes to parents

Examples of two different styles of letter writing have been given, informal and formal. Show your child a variety of your old letters pointing out the formal beginnings, 'Dear Sir' or 'Dear Madam', and 'Dear Mr' or 'Dear Mrs', and the endings. Contrast these, and the style of language, with informal letters.

13 Who's stolen the full stops?

Help! Somebody has been stealing the full stops from this page! I have put some of them back, but I need your help. Please put the other full stops back, while I track down the thief.

I went to the seaside. It was a sunny day. The sea was shiny. I had an ice cream. It was tasty I saw a crab It was red I put some shells in my bucket My mum said they were pretty I made a sandcastle I put a flag on the top

my name is sam i am five i have a little sister called judith she is funny my best friends are called ajay and harry we like to play football and ride our bikes

Tip for parents

Remind your child that names always start with a capital letter. Sentences always start with a capital letter and most end with a full stop. Sentences that are questions end with a question mark.

Question

Sam has written about himself, but he has forgotten to put in full stops and capital letters. Use a brightly coloured pen or pencil and mark them in for him.

Notes to parents

Point out punctuation to your child when you are reading together. Look at punctuation in other places, such as newspapers, comics, public notices and advertisements. Familiarise your child with the proper names for punctuation marks comma, full stop, question mark and exclamation mark.

14 Is it a question?

When a question is asked, we use a question mark like this: **?**

Look for the question marks in these sentences:

Do you like rabbits? They are my favourite animals. Do you know what they eat? Their favourite food is lettuce. Do you know what we call the house a pet rabbit lives in? We call it a hutch.

Danny is talking to Raj. Sometimes he is asking a question. Find the four questions and put in the question marks.

Is that a new scarf you are wearing I like it very much. You have got a red nose. Have you got a cold I have got some sweets to suck if your throat is sore. Would you like one The red ones are my favourites. What colour are your favourites

Activity

Write questions beginning with these question words:

what,
when,
why,
how,
where,
who.

Tip for parents

Point out question words when you are reading, so that your child learns to anticipate the correct punctuation.

Notes to parents

When you are reading questions to your child, exaggerate the 'questioning' tone in your voice to make it clear that question marks indicate the function of particular phrases or sentences.

15 Learn to spell new words

Look, Cover, Write, Check.

1. Look at the word. Look at the shape of the word. Does it have 'sticks' like **b** and **d** or any 'tails' like **p** and **y**?

   boy has a stick and a tail.

   pond starts with a tail and ends with a stick.

2. Cover the word.

3. Write the word.

4. Check the word. Is it right? If not, try again.

Question

Look at these words, then cover them, write them down and check.

dog

coat

door

mouse

Tip for parents

Learning spellings is best done in short bursts, about five minutes every day.

Notes to parents

Write out words to be learnt in large letters and encourage your child to trace the shapes of the letters with a finger. This will help your child to recall the word visually. To make a game of the activity, cut shapes out of dough or textured paper such as corrugated card or fine grade sandpaper. The sensation of 'feeling' the words will help your child to memorise them.

16 Common words

Read these words. Can you spell them?

1. had we it so with he and

2. an him the old big we at

3. be was of on here as one

4. you all what new or come get

5. call in which two for do have

6. over with that she down look because

7. they off into this out now up

8. will went me have can our only

9. would could right make then her but

10. been my not if did how where

Activity

Learn the words on this page and play the games on page 20.

Notes to parents

This list is not in any ascending order of difficulty; it serves as a list of some of the common words used regularly in the English language. Your child will meet these words frequently when reading, and will want to use them when writing. Being able to spell these words will give your child a head start, and will increase confidence about writing.

These words can be used to play the games on page 20, and can also be learned using the *Look, Cover, Write, Check* method shown on page 18. The words are divided into sets of seven to make them manageable, but if you feel your child would cope better with smaller groups of words, cut them down accordingly.

For the games, you need:
a black marker pen
stiff paper or card cut into
rectangles

Spelling games

Here are three games that you can play with your child to help with learning spellings.

Word pelmanism

Make two sets of the first word list on page 19, writing the words clearly. Shuffle the cards, then lay them face down on the floor or table. Take turns with your child to try to find the pairs of words. 'Looking' for the words intently will help your child to memorise the shape of the word. Repeat with the other word lists remembering that 'little and often' is the most effective way to learn spellings.

Word snap

Make cards in the same way as detailed above, but this time make four sets of the first word list. Play 'snap' in the usual way. Once again, the child will be concentrating on the patterns of the words in order to win the game. This will help your child to build a 'visual memory' of the words and to spell them correctly.

Repeat with the other word lists when you feel that your child is ready, remembering the 'little and often' rule.

Word chains

Lay the cards out on the floor. Start the chain with one of the words, for example:

old

Ask your child to find a word beginning with the last letter of **old** and lay it beside the first card.

Continue in the same way. The chain could, for example, grow to:

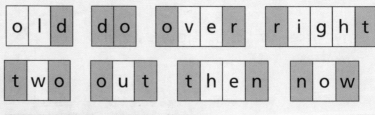

To make the game easier, work out a chain yourself and put only those cards out.

To develop the game, add cards for new words that your child learns.

17 Build a word wall

As you learn to spell these words, colour them in on the word wall.

had	we	it	so	with	he	and	an	him	the	
	old	big	we	at	be	was	of	on	here	as
one	you	all	what	new	or	come	get	call	in	
	which	two	or	do	have	over	with	that	she	down
look	where	they	off	into	this	out	now	up	will	
	want	me	have	can	our	only	would	could	right	make
then	her	but	been	my	not	if	did	how	because	

Spelling sounds

Look for the 'sounds' in words – they will help you to spell!

pen	say **p–en**	black	say **bl–ack**
had	say **h–ad**	you	say **y–ou**
for	say **f–or**		

Notes to parents

When you are helping your child to spell words, it is important that you emphasise the 'sounds' in words, rather than each individual letter, e.g. 'pen' becomes 'p-en' rather than 'p-e-n'. This will help your child as they try to build words independently.

The 'word wall' will act as a record for you to assess your child's progress. Encourage your child to learn the words and colour them on the 'bricks'. This will give a sense of achievement and will help to build confidence in spelling.

18 Letter formation

Activity

Make some labels for the things your room in your best writing.

Can you copy these letters?

⟶ = where it begins

Can you copy these words?

her   him   and   but

at   sat   you   they

Notes to parents

Your child's handwriting should be clear and legible, using regular patterns as shown in the examples above. Handwriting is generally taught at primary school level with 'flicks' on the end of appropriate letters to make the transition to 'cursive' or 'joined up' writing easier. Your child's school will have an adopted style of handwriting. Ask your child's teacher for a copy of the script, including the basic join patterns, to practise at home.

19 Handwriting practice

Can you copy this poem in the same handwriting?
It was written by a five-year-old girl who loves foxes.

Foxes, foxes in the night
With their eyes gleaming
Gleaming bright
The Farmer's enemy
That's for sure
Stealing all his
Chicken store

Notes to parents

Your child needs to practise handwriting patterns so that eventually they come naturally. This is a hard process, and we, as adults, must recognise the effort involved. (If we are tempted to forget, and become frustrated with our children, we should attempt to write neatly with the hand we are not accustomed to using. It is a great reminder!)

20 Handwriting practice

Can you copy this recipe in the same handwriting? Perhaps you will be able to make some boats of your own!

Activity

Follow the recipe and make some cheese boats.

> Potato Boats
>
> You need : 2 potatoes
> baked beans
> cheese slices
>
> Ask an adult to bake the potatoes, and cut them in half. Scoop out the potato and mash it. Mix the beans into the potato and fill the skin with the mixture. Cut the cheese slices in half. Stick a triangle on each potato boat to make a sail!

Notes to parents

This piece of handwriting is in cursive script, and the exercise should be attempted once your child has a firm grasp of correct letter formation (see page 22). Occasionally, children who encounter difficulties with 'printing' find cursive writing easier to master. You will be the best assessor of your own child's handwriting skills and should judge the right time to carry out this task. Please provide your child with wide spaced lined paper.

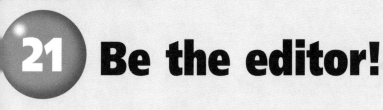

21 Be the editor!

An editor reads finished work and tries to make the piece of writing even better. Use this list to help you check your work.

1. Does your writing make sense?

2. Does your writing use exciting words?

3. Have you used full stops and capital letters?

4. Have you checked your spelling? Do the words look right? Draw a wiggly line under words that do not. Use a dictionary to check your spellings.

5. Is your handwriting neat and easy to read?

Ravinda has edited his work. His dad has helped him.

The boy jumped over the fallen log. He rushed ~~depe~~ deep into the ∧steamy jungle. He hid behind the trunk of a ~~big~~ huge tree. Suddenly, he felt something ~~going~~ slithering across his back. He gasped. What if it was a long∧ winding, snake, trying to crush him? He ~~was~~ crouched behind the tree. He was shaking∧ like a jelly He was about to scream, then something pulled his hair. He ~~terned~~ turned his head and saw a ~~little~~ tiny, bright-eyed monkey, ~~siting~~ sitting on the branch.

 **22 Story task**

Mew was only an ordinary black and white cat, but as he prowled through the grass, he imagined that he was a great jungle cat, stalking his prey. He heard a rustling sound in the crunchy leaves under the trees, and his eyes glittered.

Notes for story task

This task brings together many of the skills practised in the exercises in this book, and will check your child's understanding of the whole writing process. This task closely mirrors the method by which writing skills are assessed by your child's teacher.

Read the 'story starter' on page 26 together. Your child is going to write a short story about the cat, 'Mew'.

When you have read the 'story starter', prompt your child with some ideas about cats to write in a Brainstorm Bubble, for example, *furry, curious, hunt mice,* etc. Use a separate piece of paper for this. Look back together at page 8 to remind your child about brainstorming.

Before your child writes a story plan, look together at page 9 again.

The story should then be written as a 'first draft' or rough copy using page 26 to write on. If there is not enough space, provide extra paper. Your child can read back and add extra descriptions and interesting words to the rough copy. Check back together over pages 4 to 6 for ideas for improving the language content.

Next comes the editing stage, checking spellings and punctuation.

Finally, your child can 'publish' the finished story by copying it neatly, concentrating on handwriting. Please provide suitable paper for this. Your child may wish to include illustrations in the final copy.

Spelling test reading passage
see page 29.

This passage is for you to read to your child for the spelling test on page 29. See the *Notes to parents* on that page for instructions on conducting the test.

Sally ran through the rock pool, splashing the chilly, clear water in a shower of diamond drops.

When she reached the rocks at the far end she stopped suddenly. Partly showing through the clumps of seaweed, she **saw** something glistening in the sunlight. She peered forward for a closer **look**. It was a small **box** made of silver metal and decorated **with** blue stones. Sally picked it up. She held it to her **ear** and shook it. There was a rattling sound. Something **must** be inside, Sally thought. What **could** it be? She imagined a glittering gold coin **from** a pirate's treasure trove. Perhaps it was a ruby **ring**, once worn by a queen. Carefully, Sally opened the lid. Inside was a tiny picture frame, and in the frame was a photograph of a **boy**, standing in front of a huge castle. "**Who** is this?" Sally whispered to herself. "And how did this box get **here**?"

Picture spelling test

Together, look at the picture on page 29 and make sure your child recognises all the objects in it. Then ask your child to write the correct word in the boxes. The target words are **bird, flag, sand, ball, rock, fish, crab, shell**.

 23 Non-fiction writing task

Non-fiction writing task

1. Think of a story that you know well. Re-tell it in your own words.

2. Write a review of a book you have read.
   What can you say about the characters and what happens in the story?
   Did you like the illustrations?
   Was there anything in the book that you didn't like? Say why.

3. Your best friend is ill and has been away from school for two weeks.
   Write a letter telling your friend about things that have happened since you last saw each other.

4. Make a book. You could choose one of these topics or something else that interests you.

 The seashore    Toys    Houses and homes

Cars   Dinosaurs   My pet

5. Write the instructions for planting a bean seed in a pot. What do you need? What do you do first? Next?

Checklist

- brainstorm ideas *(page 8)*
- write a plan of questions to answer *(page 12)*
- use exciting words *(pages 4, 5, and 6)*
- check for full stops and capital letters *(page 17)*
- check spelling *(pages 20, 21 and 22)*
- do the final copy in best handwriting *(pages 24, 25, and 26)*
- draw some beautiful illustrations

Notes to parents

The tasks on this page cover the skills your child has practised through this book. The way in which your child tackles the tasks, together with the finished product, will give you an idea of your child's progress and areas that require a little more practice.

If your child chooses to make a book, help with planning, referring back to the pages indicated. Help with finding materials for illustrations and the front cover. Notes and ideas on the practical side of book making can be found on page 30.

24 Spelling and handwriting

Listen and write the words.

Sally ran through the rock pool, splashing the chilly, clear water in a shower of diamond drops. .... she reached the rocks at the far end she stopped suddenly. Partly showing through the clumps of seaweed, she .... something glistening in the sunlight. She peered forward for a closer .... It was a small .... made of silver metal and decorated .... blue stones. Sally picked it up. She held it to her .... and shook it. There was a rattling sound. Something .... be inside, Sally thought. What .... it be? She imagined a glittering gold coin .... a pirate's treasure trove. Perhaps it was a ruby ...., once worn by a queen. Carefully, Sally opened the lid. Inside was a tiny picture frame, and in the frame was a photograph of a ...., standing in front of a huge castle. "............. is this?" Sally whispered to herself. "And how did this box get ....?"

Look at the picture and write the words.

Handwriting

Choose a story that you have written yourself. Copy three sentences from it in your best handwriting.

— **Notes to parents** —

For the spelling test, see the reading passage on page 27. Read it once through to your child, who should write nothing while you read. Read it through a second time while your child follows the same passage on this page. When you come to a word in heavy type, pause, and ask your child to write that word in the space in the text. For the picture spelling test see page 27.

Making books

When children make their own books they get a great sense of achievement – and the want to read them again and again! Writing books offers children the chance t practise their writing skills and have fun at the same time.

You do not need expensive equipment or materials.
• Covers can be made from packaging covered in paper or fabric scraps.
• Pages can be made from the paper bought from toyshops for painting. It is usefu because it is thick and will be more durable than ordinary paper.

To fix the pages inside the covers, you can:
• staple the pages inside the cover, (put sticky tape over the staples to protec little fingers);
• use a hole punch or a sharp, thick needle to make holes in the cover and the pape Tie the pages together with a shoelace, thick yarn, ribbon or metal binder rings.

Folding books

When making a folding book, ask your child to write each page of the story on pieces of paper a little smaller than the folding book. Stick the pieces of paper onto the pages of the folding book. If your child makes a mistake in writing, the work can be repeated on a single piece of paper. You will also have a coloured border to each page.

Use a long strip of stiff paper, coloured, if possible. Stick several pieces together wit glue or tape until you have the desired length. Fold the strip in accordian fashion int equal sized pages, with the first page opening as a conventional book.

A stiff piece of card can be stuck onto the first page to make a cover the same size a the book.

You can make shaped covers for the front and back. Tape them onto the folded car pages.

Flap book

These are a great motivator due to the 'surprises' under the flaps!
Simply tape one edge of the flap over the illustration or words that form the surprise.

Ideas for 'lift the flap' books
Who's knocking at the door?
Who's been eating this leaf?
What's in my pocket?
What's in the box?

Who's been eating this leaf? A caterpillar

GLOSSARY

author
(Page 11) a person who writes books

brainstorming
(Page 8) collecting ideas to put in a story or a piece of writing

character
(Page 11) a person in a story

editor
(Page 25) a person who reads finished work and improves it

fiction
(Page 12) story books

full stop (.)
(Page 16) the dot that marks the end of a sentence

illustration
(Page 25) a picture in a book

illustrator
(Page 25) a person who draws pictures for a book

non-fiction
(Page 12) information books

punctuation
(Page 25) the marks used in writing to help it make sense

question mark (?)
(Page 17) the sign at the end of a sentence that shows it is a question

sentence
(Page 16) a group of words that make sense and express a single idea

story plan
(Page 9) a short description of what is in the story: the characters, where the story happens, what happens, how it begins and ends

title
(Page 11) what a book or story is called

ANSWERS

Page 4

Suggested answers

flower – pretty, colourful, bright, beautiful, scented, soft

Page 6

Suggested answers

Not just BIG but – gigantic, massive, enormous

Not just LITTLE but – minute, small, teeny, weeny

Not just SAD but – miserable, tearful, gloomy, glum, upset

Not just HAPPY but – glad, delighted, cheerful

Question

nasty, awful, bad, disgusting

Page 16

Who's stolen the full stops?

I went to the seaside. It was a sunny day. The sea was shiny. I had an ice cream. It was tasty. I saw a crab. It was red. I put some shells in my bucket. My mum said they were pretty. I made a sandcastle. I put a flag on the top.

Question

My name is Sam. I am five. I have a little sister called Judith. She is funny. My best friends are called Ajay and Harry. We like to play football and ride our bikes.

Page 17

Is it a question?

Is that a new scarf you are wearing? I like it very much. You have got a red nose. Have you got a cold? I have got some sweets to suck if your throat is sore. Would you like one? The red ones are my favourites. What colour are your favourites?

Page 21

th–at

c–an

Page 29